The Escape To Everywhere

Based On Early Talks From
The Incomplete Works Of

Paul Hedderman

☙

Transcribed and Edited By

James Saint Cloud

Let It Be Publishing
San Rafael, California

ISBN   0692346783

ISBN-13: 978-0692346785
(Let It Be Publishing)

LET IT BE PUBLISHING, SAN RAFAEL, CALIFORNIA

4460 Redwood Highway, Suite 16-227
San Rafael, California 94903 USA

Cover photograph by Don Moseman

In Memoriam

Jim Cooke. 1931 - 2014

When your practices themselves become a means of giving life to the non- existent thing, how can they destroy it?

--- Sri Ramana

Editor's Note:

This material is drawn primarily from Paul's Saturday morning talks in San Francisco and Mill Valley, California.

Please come by if you're in the area; there's no charge but a hat gets passed. Maybe even your hat!

The speaking schedule (also coming to a country near you) is on Paul's web site:

Zenbitchslap.com

There's some repetition here, which I invite you to consider as a spiral into concepts till they're no longer new.

Travel light!

James Saint Cloud

Mill Valley, California
rumistories @ yahoo.com

How can a solution work on an imaginary problem?
The ' solution' is to recognize it's imaginary.
The quickest way out is to realize you're not in.

--- Paul

The Escape To Everywhere

Based On Early Talks From
The Incomplete Works Of

Paul Hedderman

Each moment Life streams through the gates of the senses, fresh and new. That's CONSCIOUS CONTACT.

Then the mind hijacks it, saying, "I am what's in conscious contact. I am doing the seeing, touching, thinking."

The mind's modus operandi is CLAIMING. There is life and it's happening; then the mind claims that life. Now life is happening to me.

A bird flies by. There is simple consciousness of it. Seeing happens. Then the head says, "I saw that."

WHO is seeing --- the sense of being the one seeing --- becomes more important than SEEING itself. The conscious contact is being claimed by the head. It puts you to sleep to the awareness that you ARE the conscious contact.

"Selfing" is parasitic. It's taken over. You may be looking FROM it all day.

What's looking is what you're looking for.

--- Saint Francis of Assisi

Life is a VERB. It's just happening. Not TO anyone. Just energy, riffing like crazy. Selfing makes a NOUN of itself. A thing through body-identification.

The illusion of being a noun is that everything is happening from outside TO YOU. All day, every bit of conscious contact that is continually happening, your head is claiming it, as YOU (the body) being the one in contact.

But the "self" is just a story the mind's running. Nothing ever happened to what I AM. I am the pure and simple AWARENESS of events.

Life is happening; it's a verb. The verb is the reality and the noun is the illusion. You are looking at it from the point of view of being a noun so you're missing it.

That's what your head is doing all day: INTERPRETING what is going on and making it into a story about something else. You lose the verbing of life as soon as the noun claims the experience as something that happened to it.

You can drop down into verbing and see the noun in action. See it on its throne. The verbing doesn't stop; it's always on. There is not a "past of presence" nor a "future of presence." There is BEING. Now.

Awareness is the CONTEXT of life. What you incorrectly call "self" is a CONTENT.

Planes don't bump into the sky. "Hey, I almost hit some sky." No. Rain comes, the sky doesn't get wet. Fireworks go off. But the sky remains the same.

Take a bowl. Put things in it; make soup. Does the bowl change? No, no more than the bowl of sky does when the birds and stars move through. No more than the mind does as thoughts flow in and out. This emptiness the mind is so afraid of --- this is really HOME.

You ARE that SPACE, entertaining the conscious awareness of what's appearing each moment. But you identify with a mental process that says, "I am in the soup."

"Why is life happening to me this way?" Because you've construed yourself as a part of the soup when you're really the context, the bowl. Life seems to be happening TO you, as the soup, a whole drama of not enough spice and so on. You see life's content but miss the context in which it's held --- the freedom that is 'prior to' the self. You see the stars but give little attention to the sky in which they're held. We love the movie, yet never clap for the screen.

The ego uses seeking as a stratagem to hide your true identity. It knows you won't "find" what you already are!

The bowl has a purpose: It holds. You ARE that space. The conscious space that is aware and conscious of what's appearing in it. Holding all the appearances that are happening as they pass. But we've identified with a mental process that says "I" am part of the content, floating around in the soup. The soup is happening to me.

Your life becomes a storage unit full of mental memorabilia, past and future thought --- though life is NOW with thoughts passing each moment freely through.

You're in the soup, thinking that's what you are as you stir the thoughts and feelings that fill the bowl. You do not have awareness, awareness has you.

There has to be an application of new glue every day to rebind your mind to the idea of your being a self. Because it's all smoke and mirrors. The makings of selfing can only reach the level of "seemingly so."

The mind is selfing all day long, and in that mirror of selfing there is the appearance of a "you." Mirror, mirror, mirror, making up an appearance of something real. An aspect of mind has become identified with that appearance, and it has become lost in the world of mirrors. And it's trying to get out. But self can't get out of self. The whole point is to recognize you're not self.

There is an activity of mind working on appearance. Trying to make the appearance better. All the appearances have one faulty point: They're not real. (Though the space that they are appearing in is real.)

What happens when you stop taking marching orders from thought? Self is no longer in the center. There is a shift as the 'my' comes out.

The body becomes the focal point of this ruse. MY body. MY this, MY that. See how much heavier the thoughts become with the 'my' thrown in!

Will you put Life into so small a cage, like a small bird? It's the nature of the bird to fly. When it becomes YOUR bird you have a caged bird. Is it truly a bird now anymore?

Out at the rim of the bowl (outside the content) life waits, always available. There you realize the thoughts are not you. They are passing, like the birds. Simple witnessing, as the eye would witness a passing bird: That's conscious contact.

Do you follow the birds home, to peer into the bowl of their nest? Then why do it with the thoughts?

Being a self is an exhausting job! Why grasp at life? Release all that! Set attention free — be a hawk high overhead.

As Jesus says, "You're in the world but not of it." We're in the soup but not part of it. That makes it easy to swim in the soup, realizing you're not "of" it.

It's not so much that we are IN conscious contact; we ARE the conscious contact.

You're conscious of things through the body's instrument. There's five gates of consciousness in the body: Your relationship to things. The head reacts to that conscious contact and says, "I'm seeing, I'm feeling," and so on. The next step after that is an interpretation: Conscious contact being interpreted from the point of view of self-centeredness.

The self claims the consciousness of tasting, hearing, touching, thinking, and off it goes. Spinning off from that point, all day every day. Taking the conscious contact and running with it.

The conscious contact is the Life-Giving of All Life. That's the only way you know you have your life, because you're conscious to what's flowing each moment through the five gates. Life is happening, all of it right now. But our interpretation is, life is happening to ME: self-centeredness.

There's no peace in an agitated mind. A swell on the water produced by heavy winds of false evidence, breaking over and over on itself.

But when there's an entertaining, "I'm not that," you can experience a pause, a timeless moment in a linear time frame. That's a pause you can live in. Live AS. It's not something you can attain. It's always available.

It's a whole different way of traveling. If you don't see false evidence as true, how will there be anxiety?

You've got to see what this mind entertains. It entertains that if something is good it's going to end quickly. When it's bad it's going to last forever. The entertaining is unbelievable! The task it has been put to is what's driving it crazy.

We're entertaining time. We think there's a future. Can you land in the future? Is there an airport there? But you seem to be landing there everyday. Head. Mental experience. That little alley, the dead end of the conditioned mind that can only go backward and forward.

What's the solution to WHAT'S NOT HAPPENING? It's really simple. Very, very clean. You don't have to sign up for a subscription. Don't have to re-up it. You don't have to go on a retreat for it. Don't have to get in on an installment plan. The solution to what's not happening is recognizing it's not happening. If you recognize it's not happening, all desire to provide a solution to it is snuffed out; because you realize it's not happening. It takes no time at all.

A simple recognition! Then your attention goes where? To WHAT IS HAPPENING. Now you're present. And what you get off on actually is YOU, BEING PRESENT. Not what's happening so much as you, being here. It's a simple message.

As soon as self starts managing, life becomes unmanageable.

Self-centeredness is what's managing. There is no you that's managing; it's a mental program called self-centeredness that's reacting to everything that comes up in awareness.

Awareness is what's happening — conscious contact, the direct interface with the moment. But there's a mental reaction to what's happening that overrides the conscious contact, so that you spin out in a story about what's happening. Adding chapter after chapter to apply solutions; and you don't see that "problem and solution" is the bigger problem.

You're not aware that your true life is conscious contact. Your reactions are based on being a body, a separate-long-lasting-independent-entity, so that all your reactions are based on ignorance. If your life story is told from this point of view it is going to be very confusing for you. It's not going to translate into happiness, joy, and freedom when you accept everyone else's formulae about how to be happy, joyous, and free. All based on the false assumption of this body-identification.

What fuels the selfing is your attention to the thoughts, your obsession with them. But the thoughts are about a body, not about you. Seeing that, you can become disinterested in it.
The energy gets freed up. Maybe you'll even become interested in the source of life, consciousness.

You think you're separate from life and it's HAPPENING TO you. "I'm the noun that everything is happening to."

But there is no noun in living; it's just verbing.

When you're seeing with a noun way of looking you are interpreting life from a false center. And you don't understand why you're so confused.

All the experiences of verbing become something that the noun HAD.

You're wanting the verb-ness of life, but you're missing it. You're saddled with this noun way of looking at things. There is the dilemma: You cannot see you've made yourself into a noun, for you look at everything from a noun's perspective. The noun cannot get the sense of peace because peace is a living movement, not a stagnant thing you acquire or capture.

As a noun life becomes interpreted and you become a storage unit for the mind's interpretation of life. You're not experiencing a living moment, you're rehashing an old moment. You live from memory; interpretation is constantly presented to override the living-ness of life.

As a noun the best you can do is to assume that you HAD an experience; you cannot be THAT in which the experience occurs. One is a movement; the other is a package deal. You're either moving with things or you are packaging them up, "I know this and that; I've had this and that experience." Taking the verb and transforming it into something you possess.

The mind's interpretation is, "All right, I'm going to stick myself in front of that verb. Stick myself in as a noun and edit life, under the assumption that I am the doer of this verb. I am seeing, I am touching, I am feeling, I am hearing, and I am especially thinking about it all. The doer and the haver and the interpreter.

Exhausting! Trying to have control over it all. Grasping at some assurance it's going to be okay down the river. Building dams and reservoirs

You assume you are in a box. Three sides in front of you, and your body is the fourth side. A little box of self-centeredness with only a certain amount of possibility for it, re-hashing the same old aspirations and the same old maps to what seems to be a well but has no water.

You can look behind you, at the back of the box, what you called the fourth wall. This thing called Paul — this wall isn't a wall. You see it's not a true box; the thing you thought was restraining you doesn't exist.

When light meets light there's no reaction to it. That's the pause. And it's never-ending. You get broken from the bondage of self when the light is turned upon itself. Your reactions change. Something that would get your hackles up won't anymore. Not a slave to situations and circumstances any more; there's immunity to it now. The Mind reflects consciousness and sees itself.

The self can't get rid of the consciousness or erase it, so it claims it. And in so doing the mind seemingly forgets what it is. That's what the mind does. It seems to cause unconsciousness. What an incredible feat for the mind to do that!

Whatever the mind presents, just rest in the seeing of it. Don't react. Then you'll have immunity to what the mind presents. Your reactions will change and life will be different. Because it's your reaction that gives life its meaning. Life is "what's happening." But when it's a mental reaction, it's "what's happening to me."

We are "what" is seeing, not the "who" that's looking.

Self-centeredness is a failed program.

You're the projector of the thing called life. Then the meaning gets funneled through self-centeredness, looking at life as "how it pertains to me."

The attention is captured by self-centeredness. Like water that's been bottled. It uses the captured attention to fuel the bondage of self.

Let's say agitation occurs. What reacts to it is the self-centeredness. The reaction to the discomfort is the idea it is imposing itself "on you."

The self-centeredness tries to manage it. It asks, "What can I do to change it?" The solutions the self-centeredness applies then represent an even bigger problem. Self clicks in and a whole story ensues. You blame someone. You act out. You have a ten year prison sentence.

This is MY girlfriend; I have a right to know where she is. There's anger, coming from self-centeredness. So you get to be alone and right, when what you wanted was love. Your head's reaction causes you to get the opposite of what you wanted. Self's reaction creates a world of problems called solutions.

What is possible is a moment of pause to allow another program to come in, one called a higher power. A response that does not produce a long list of problems.

Most of us are reacting to what's not happening.

Your head may be in next Friday. Your body will be reacting as if next Friday is more important than today. Maybe you're getting fired next Friday. You're having a preemptive reaction to it, consumed with what's not happening. Does it help? No. It overrides your ability to respond to what IS happening.

All you need to entertain is What Is Happening — and phew! You're back.

Huge mental catacombs can be erased in one second if you only acknowledge what IS happening — acknowledgment of the awareness itself.

To the head, not having a clue is very not-okay. It feels it has safety by knowing things.

But you can't "know life" as separate from you, as though under glass to study it. You can only live it. Wanting to "know it" takes the heart out of it.

Zen talks about this "not knowing" state. HERE is what's going on. If your head doesn't like it, so what? Break through that idea that nothing's happening in the moment. There's a lot happening! That, to me, is the relief of all reliefs.

You entertain you're the doer; and when you entertain you're the doer you can entertain being guilty and shameful about what you did and didn't do.

When I was a kid my father used to play with me like fathers do. Then when I turned six he got sick, very sick, so he stopped playing with me. I am sure they sat me down, the older relatives, saying, "Listen Paul, your father is sick, that's why he's not playing with you."

Self-centeredness said I had to have had something to do with it. I had done something for my father to choose not to play with me. That is, bottom line, the only way I saw it. I was self centered, so everything was basically, somehow, always based on me; so his not playing with me had to do with me.

That's what the mind entertains in self-centredness. You become the root cause of many things you have nothing to do with.

All the guilt people are feeling and dumping on others is that guilt of separation they believe they must have caused. Why? Because that's the only way self centeredness thinks. It sees everything as how it pertains to it. Based on something you did or didn't do.

Now sit with that and see how unbearable that is. And what is the mind going to do with that unbearability? Dump it, project it, blame others! All these ways to get relief from its own pollution.

The selfing is one of the worst mental pollutants of all. The way it processes this place does not work. It produces so much refuse and garbage and then you meet another person, maybe someone who is your significant other, and that's the place you think is the dump so you pull your truck up and dump.

"I'm looking for my prince, someone to share my life with." You're not even enjoying your life! Why would you want to bring another person into the mix?

Seriously. Someone to entertain me in my prison cell. You have this incredible home entertainment center; but it's still a prison.

The mental process keeps representing the limited possibilities, and the captivated mind is like a marathon runner running laps in a little four by four foot closet. It's just unbelievable.

If everything is being entertained from the self of the mental process that's entertaining 'you' all day — that's truly enslavement.

The mind is constantly entertaining this ('you') and as such it is entertaining very limited possibilities. You know it! In such entertaining, the possibility of being okay here is always, 'Okay, 'I' <u>will</u> be okay'. In such entertaining, being okay is always based on time and what you do or don't do or what somebody else does or doesn't do. The possibility of being saved is based on a seeming bondage.

When what we are waiting for fails to deliver satisfaction the mind produces excuses, rationales, and blame. The mental process has to cover up the fact that it's inadequate in bringing you what you are looking for. Which is what? Peace of mind! It cannot bring you peace because peace is inherently in the Mind — but not when it is agitated and identified with the mental process.

So, we are trying to find peace of mind by discovering the source of agitation to the mind **when the mind is the agitation.**

You can't get there as a seeker. See, that's the selfing.

You are identified as something that you're not.

What gives value to the journey? The real value (consciousness) can't be entertained by the self so there has to be the pot of gold at the end of the spiritual rainbow. Then there's doing and having as that is the only modality the self knows. It seems spirit as an experience it can have.

The prior nature has seemingly been overridden by this insinuated nature. The mind cannot entertain THAT as you because you are already busily entertaining THIS (the body) as you. So it makes its own nature an object to seek for.

But what if, just possibly, I'm not this mental construct I'm seemingly looking from all day?

You say you want to be "awake."

But while you are adsorbed in the story of self you will be unconscious to the fact that you are ALREADY AWAKE. Then you may have the curse of thinking you want to BECOME awake. Reinforcing the idea that you are not awake, so on and so on.

The head is playing God. And it's already beat you, since now it's got you thinking you're not awake. It's going to play with that for years. The true happening is awareness; and that's always happening. The relief you are seeking is always available. You don't have to go into therapy, work on your fears and phobias, no; just realize you're not that which needs to be therapized.

When you wake from the dream there's an instant recognition: It's a dream-tiger. The dream is not happening. In most cases your anxieties are a product of what's not happening.

See it as a line of knots. You read books and go to therapists. But if you undo the first knot, the misidentification with what is not, it loosens all the other knots.

You'll travel lighter. You'll just know; they'll be an unspoken "yes." You can recognize consciousness through the presence of awareness.

There's no escaping WHAT'S SO. You can SENSE living or else you can THINK about it. That's the choice.

We are trapped into believing we ARE A THING.
There's the dilemma: The act of identifying as the body.

You don't need a map to go to the truth. You are the truth! Consciousness is inherently available to us. That's it. That's the way.

Truth is available at all times, but it's not available to WHAT YOU'RE NOT. What you're not will never access it, it's impossible.

Your head believes you're what you're not and causes you to be unconscious of the consciousness.

But there's no you that's going through the door, because there is no you. The idea of being a you creates the idea of a door to the truth that's always out of reach.

The idea that you might suddenly meet up with the truth? No! You are that truth. You are consciousness, right now.

The curse of "spiritual seeking" may take you on a journey to become conscious of consciousness? How's that going to work?

Any time self gets revealed not to be you, it will regroup. Even if there's a great epiphany, self takes credit for it. Blown into bits, self forms again. The head will arise and say, "I had this great experience." Neutering the whole point of the epiphany: A message of life unadorned by self.

Now you have epiphanies to put on your spiritual resume. Antlers on the mantle. Moving right up there.

Suppose you notice you've been on a train of thought. That noticing is the pause. Stay in the pause! There's no need to react to the thought. If you notice the thought's not "yours" you'll stay in the pause and not react. Not beholden to it. The pause is the field. The NO THING that interfaces. The universal subjectivity that's looking through us.

Whatever the mind presents, just **rest in what's seeing it** and you'll have immunity to what the mind presents. Your reactions will change and life will be totally different, because **it's your reaction that gives it meaning.** Life is "what's happening." When it's a reaction, it's "what's happening to me."

The "you" represents a lot of old ideas. Thousands of files of built-in conditioning --- the idea this is happening TO Paul. The files are downloaded and give meaning to what's happening, so that Paul's reaction to this conditioned state and all that arises is met with a reaction from an artificial state instead of a sense of the consciousness of the moment. I **get an interpretation of the moment**, from the point of view of Paul's files. I'm being driven by that interpretation.

When I was a kid playing there was only awareness, interfaced with life, consciousness of what was happening.

Then I grew out of that state. Through introspection a neurosis set in. All the confusion and discomfort related to being a self came about. The idea I knew something. A bogus knowledge. The self, the seat of artificial knowing, claimed the knowledge. "I have this knowledge." Neutering it.

The conscious contact had been forgotten; the conditioning had taken its place. Then the excitement I used to have as a child simply running out the door, all that changed; I had to do bungee jumping to even get a glimpse of it. Shock therapy to feel that I'm alive. That's not being alive. It's living an interpretation by a program of the head called self-centeredness.

The knowledge of not knowing a freakin' thing — that sets you free. Not having a clue. No idea. **Like a vast infinite field right behind the noggin.** Not knowing what's flying in and going out. **That state of unknowing is the space.**

It isn't about, "Now I've got to live in the state of unknowing." No. It doesn't matter if you worry about next week or not. Just find out who is it that's worrying!

Instead of dealing with all its effects, let's go to the root of it and see if you're that. If you're not that, I tell you, your interest will be freed from it, to go other places. Maybe to harvest love and peace rather than fear and resentment and the need to be right.

I'm saying, the dilemma that you're in is linked into being the long-lasting independent separate entity.

You have a lot of faith. Only not in the right vehicle. If you have faith that what's NOT happening IS happening, there will be a lot of anxiety about what could have or should be happening.

Watch people who have faith in their thoughts. They're a wreck. Not here for all intents and purposes. Their thoughts don't abide here, they abide in time. Worshiping time. Worried. Reminiscing. Out to lunch.

They have total faith; they believe in every thought their minds provide. That's the false evidence that appears true. "What? Not be concerned about what might happen to me?"

If faith is in the "I don't know," there's comfort in your own skin. It's very simple here. It's just so. False evidence doesn't take birth here. It's not lent action with the resulting unfortunate results.

A sense of being HERE provides an immunity to the "mental here." You don't get rid of the self. Because it was never there. You sense the appearance of a mental construct called selfing. But self was never there. There is no self. No reason to get rid of it. That's the solution!

The selfing infers, assumes, implies, and swears. All empty pointing to "the imagined one." The mind through identification leaps from the pointing to the pointed. The bondage of self.

You see what's being presented as "you" through thought and interpretation of feelings; and you can question that assumption by the head.

"All right, so where is this 'you'?" You ask subjective questions. "Who am I? What is this life? If I'm not the doer of this life, whose is it anyway?" Sit there, pause, see what happens, yeah? The deck may be shuffled.

But there's no "getting rid of it." The best way to get out of it is to realize you're not in it. This place is a dualistic trap. That's how the split mind works, comparing opposites. We try to decide where we fit in to that. Problem, solution. Again, again. That's the slavery here. You want out of the problem? Entertain this idea: You were never in the problem.

The bigger problem is being bound to self's reactions to life rather than living.

The act of identifying keeps the bondage intact. Then the revelation: I'm not that. Then when you take a look at self's expressions they don't have a hold on you! The obsessing stops.

Learn about self from the point of view of being free of it, not continuing to obsess. You can be fearless about self. Because it's not you!

Selfing is open ended, there's no closure. If you deal with all your Earthly problems your mind will still make up a few on Mars.

Ever new crops of problems for you to be enthralled by and work through. "Oh, I'm getting better, working through these problems."

The real goal is freedom from self. The one dilemma for most people is that they've never heard the solution. Well now you've been served the spiritual subpoena.

Can you respond to this ability to be free? It's available. The tight tunnel vision will open up. There's a grand vista once the blinders come off. You'll start breathing space and peace instead of fear and anxiety.

Just now your lungs are contracted in the fear of impending doom. Totally coiled up. Once you start breathing this you'll expand in a natural response to "what's happening."

The energy given to self centeredness becomes a reaction. The energy given to life becomes a response.

The energy given to self centeredness fuels a seeker, a getter, a proprietor, a privatizer.

The energy given to "this" becomes an expresser, a dancer, an extender. Not taking, taking, taking. You live by giving it away. You don't have anything so you don't entertain losing it.

You'll intimate some of Nature's qualities. This incessant on-ness. What was separated is put together. Like having a new set of glasses. A 3-D movie, with the glasses suddenly on. A sense of being alive. Consciousness; rather than being so enthralled with what I'm conscious of.

Once you taste the relief, all you can do is laugh.

A lot of people simply want to be better, just as they are. They want to become A BETTER SELF.

They don't realize that **the idea of being a self is what is causing the bondage**; it's not happening from an outside source.

Self-centeredness binds you to things, and a meaning is given to those things so that they affect you. Circumstances don't bind you; the self centeredness binds you to the circumstances.

This is "selfing." If you do somehow get relief from outside situations you're going to need to get even more relief from the outside situations, because the bonding agent isn't on the outside, but the inside.

We never entertain the idea of being outside the realm of self-centeredness, because it's taken root in us and we are identified with it. So all we can do is therapize and socialize it so it doesn't flip out at the next picnic. We just hunker down in the chronic effects of self-centeredness. Failing to see the self as the parasite that it is.

But then, instead of seeing from it all day, you can see IT. When you see it you can be free of it. It's really the freedom from the bondage of self we're looking for. The bondage of self is not from outside, it's from inside; you're the bonding agent.

Self lives in a world of dualistic possibilities that are not correct.

It believes it can become spiritual, but inherently it is not spiritual. I can feel peace or get peace but I can also lose the peace. I feel connected, and I also feel disconnected. It entertains possibilities based on duality. That's what it does.

But in fact, the conscious contact is choiceless, simply what's happening. An interpretation of the conscious contact includes the idea that it's possible to be in it or out of it. Which is a lie.

Your mind is just reacting. We forget that we ARE conscious contact; then there's trouble, because life is no longer seen as what is simply happening, but is seen as what is happening TO ME. We call this normal everyday activity. But it's just selfing. Selfing selfing selfing.

I have opinions about this and that. I want what's happening to that person over there instead of what's happening to me. And so on. It's an insane point of view. The more attention is absorbed by selfing the less I'm aware of the conscious contact. Less attentive, more prone to interpretation.

Your attention orbits around the planet Self all day, because the self provides the gravitational pull to all the thoughts, making them about YOU.

If you realized they weren't about the real you, they could simply come and go. Your attention would be freed up from the slavery of selfing and would attend to the conscious contact; there would be a recognition in and of itself. Traveling lighter — not by any procedures or practice, simply by recognition of what is so. You don't add anything to it or subtract anything, just become conscious of it. You're already that.

If you recognize you're not the self you will lose interest in all its activities, the processes that facilitate it. The reason I'm hooked on the narrative in my head is because I think it's about me. By freeing the attention from the selfing we become aware of the conscious contact, the enslavement is over.

Let's simply entertain that we may not be the selfing.

Then you'll lose interest in obsessing with the thoughts, making up stories about the feelings you're having or not having. The attention that's glued to the screen of selfing will be released. Will go back to the conscious contact, each moment's raw experience.

Get a better self? When will that be delivered? Never now. Always put off.

"When I arrive there, it will all be great." And when you arrive? The happiness doesn't arrive; and the mind blames you for it.

Selfing is not what you are. There is no noun happening. But when you look into the past, or look into the future, it's all about what is happening to the self. It can worry the hell out of you. Faith in the mental projections produces the anxiety.

Solution: Look at a situation and see no problem. Only what is now. Being-ness. With that recognition comes immunity from becoming a noun. The real flavor of life, just happening — not happening "to me" — this is the open secret, the gateless gate. Available at all times.

Realize you're not in the problem. Never have been. That's the solution. The lie is that you were "in self." But you never were. Your attention was hijacked, that's all.

The lie is that there is someone that was in self, or out of self. There has never been anyone in, so how could there be anyone out.

Self-centeredness leads to fear, since self-centeredness is unreliable.

Faith in self produces the anxiety that you try to deal with as though the anxiety is real and solid. The same faith put into the infinite will create an ease and comfort. Travelling lighter.

The mind tries to write its relevance into the story. But things are just happening. It has nothing to do with the self at all. The head's interpretation is causing travel to be very heavy. All based on the idea of being a self.

Self says it wants to "be free," but true freedom is to be free OF IT: To be the verb of attention, pure and freed from self.

Selfing needs attention; when the attention is taken from it, there is the freedom.

Self reliance is unreliable. Its whole foundation rests on false assumptions. For example: "If only this had happened then everything would be great. What happened didn't have to happen. Yesterday and tomorrow are more important than now. I have a lot to do with things I have nothing to do with."

You need a three-day retreat. Why? To have a story? "Now I'm a spiritual person."

Consciousness has become a commodity you trade, like stocks. Based on what we do as the "doer." We make commerce of it. We sense that we enlarge and contract.

But how can a body ever become spiritual? It's always going to become spiritual as a body. That defeats the whole purpose. If you are spirit, why is there any need to become spiritual? You already are!

As a body it seems, "If I become spiritual, it will bring advantage. So let me try grafting some spirit onto me. I'll listen to talks by the masters and do some study."

When you're sensing the presence of yourself, that's the absence of truth, literally.

When you sense this (slapping the body) as being absent, that's presence. It takes absolutely no time, there's no practice, no debate. It's obvious. It's the sense of the absence of you.

If you believe you did something to get this you definitely believe you could do something to lose it.

Or the other way around: "Well, I didn't do enough today to feel it." You'd be playing god all freakin' day.

Perhaps you have an epiphany: An event of life with the absence of self. You get the flavour of the moment, life-as-it-happens, and it startles the self into submission. The self goes down, goes to its corner, has some water thrown on it; but it's soon back in the ring again, saying, "Oh! I HAD the experience, this epiphany!" It pulls out a victory from the jasws of defeat.

Generally the epiphany ends when this selfing arises and interpretation begins. A couple of epiphanies like that and you'll be a spiritual noun. Ha-ha!

The epiphany is an event. Then there is the mind's reaction to it. Claiming it. The mind says, "I, this long-lasting independent separate entity, just had this spiritual experience." Yes? It just neutered the whole event by claiming it. The epiphany was not an experience you had, it was the absence of the selfing!

The heavens open up. The mental process has been stunned into stopping. Did you make a reservation for it? Did you call up ahead of time? Put on the right music for the event?

No. It just burst through, interrupting your linear story of life as a noun, your sense of being a historical action figure.

And the epiphany can offer a glimpse outside the box —
a portal between timeless and time I call the "pause" or
the "gap." At that moment there was only awareness.
The moment was set free again, out of its box.

Attention gets out of the box and spreads out. An
eternal non-time event in this linear story of time.
Witnessing seeing, feeling, touching, tasting, and
thinking as the eye would witness a bird going by
overhead. That's conscious contact.

You are spirit. Your interface here is through a body. The body is only a conveyance.

You look through a telescope to see the stars and the stars seem to come closer. In the same way consciousness comes through the lenses of our senses to experience the world.

Consciousness gets to see, feel, taste, touch this place. Talk about an amusement park! It's a total surround experience.

Consciousness is the subject moving through this object of the body. Then the object has a mental process in which it claims itself to be the subject.

What an incredible responsibility to be burdened with! All that attention is like a giant spotlight and you just can't handle it.

It's like when you were a kid investigating an insect with a magnifying glass. You don't know the effect the sun has and you burn the poor little thing up. All you wanted to do was know it. And all you want to do is know "you" but you burn the head to death, because that attention magnified through the self-centeredness, the identification with self, is much too much for you.

All day instead of having what life presents, your head re-presents it. You go over it and over it with all these assumed superpowers, such as, "It could have been different if this or that." Those are like doors to hell.

When you see the door and it says, "If only," don't go there!

"I should have," and, "I shouldn't have." You can get lost in there for a long time.
The head re-presents your life as though you are a God that could change it. Doesn't it? Why would you think about something that was unchangeable, with a feeling that you could change it by thinking about it? Why would your head dwell on something that was unchangeable unless it believed it had the power to change it? Contrary to all the evidence that that activity presents, it keeps on keeping on. Re-presenting life as though it could be different.

The re-presenting is based on the idea that you believe you have power. That things could be different. That is a constant denial of things as they are.

Acceptance of what-is is the easiest activity of all. What is it that I need to change if I'm in acceptance? Absolutely nothing. Everything is totally okay as it is.

There's no effort or thought on your part in acceptance. That's traveling lighter. That's the freedom. Not a freedom five years from now or when you graduate, but a freedom applicable each moment. You travel not with it, but AS it.

Consciousness is the lightest thing of all. It's no-thing, yet it touches on everything. You wouldn't have any sense of anything that appears here without that no-thing. It's the lightest of all lightness. It just knows. It can't be located, it can't be quantified, can't be captured, and can't expire. It's always SO at all times.

People go to the top of the Empire State building and look through the telescopes at the scene below. I don't believe any of them walk away with the impression of BEING the telescope.

But that's what self does, identifying consciousness with the apparatus, the telescope. A mental process constantly reinforced with that daily narrative of you as this body and mind. It's all about you.

But you're not even the camera. You're just a tripod! Being repositioned here and there for the view of consciousness, for it to see, feel, taste, touch.

We're telling the story of life based on being the tripod. "I'm in a really good position, I'm in Pacific Heights. Much better than that position at Sixth and Market."

But the camera's just seeing as it always does.

It's the simple recognition of what's so.

Thoughts are like corn kernels, and you're the popcorn maker.

There is heat and they begin to pop, and you become aware of them. For a while the thoughts are just what's happening, like trains going by. Then you inject all this buttery goo, making it about YOU. That's when things get sticky.

Feelings and thoughts do not bring you any meaning. You are injecting them with meaning. How do you do that? By making it MY thought and MY feeling.

You open up the thought or the feeling as though it BROUGHT you the meaning; though the meaning is already in the files, downloading through the me and my.

Let's say I have a belief that I'm lazy. The thought comes, "I haven't done anything today." It could just pass. But I think it's about ME. Then all these meanings download from my files. I follow it on the screen and it takes me into a story into the mystical place in which Paul is really bad, where Paul hasn't done anything in his whole life and has no value whatsoever. It's a trip into WHAT'S NOT HAPPENING.

People who go to Hawaii come back with a tan. But I go on this train trip to what's not happening. I go on mental trips and come back with anxiety, recrimination, and shame. The trip's about ME and I have a great interest in it. Why? Because I'm identified with it all.

The freedom comes when you lose interest in the dilemmas. How do you lose interest? By entertaining the simple message, "I'm not that."

You simply witness what is. Something shows up, and after that something else. A thought or feeling comes into awareness, does its little acrobatic act, then the circus packs up and leaves. Then you're conscious of the next event, and the next. It's a very smooth clean way of living, yes? Very fluid.

Most humans are living in that world of WHAT'S NOT HAPPENING. Living in THE THOUGHT OF past and future. This produces a lot of anxiety. "What might happen to me?"

The physical apparatus is reacting to that. Being stressed by living more than one day at a time.

You worry about what you will be like 20 years from now. But you will have a whole different personality then. **You are worrying for a complete stranger.** You're not going to be anything like what you are now. Are you what you were projecting yourself to be when you were a kid? You're not that person.

You can recognize when a journey to What's Not Happening is underway. That recognition is your relief.

The activity of trains is not to stay at the station; they come and go. They pick up passengers and they take them somewhere. But you are the central station, the awareness, through which the trains constantly come in and go out.

In a while, if you don't get engaged in the contents, you may become engaged in the CONTEXT — in the consciousness of what's WITNESSING everything showing up — the station — instead of getting on the trains of thoughts and feelings being used by selfing to carry you away.

When you're identified as a long-lasting independent separate entity it makes you a passenger at that station. Your drive is to get on a train in the hope that it's going to take you somewhere. You have hopes and expectations and conditional desires that society has built into you, with the hope of arriving somewhere by doing or having. Having two kids and a picket fence and so on.

These trains will come and we get on them and we call them the journey of life. Sometimes the trains are locals to a heaven, and the next stop is to a hell, and it goes on like that.

Now in a sense all of these thoughts and all of these feelings and all the experiences you have everyday have been anchored into being by one act and one act only:

Consciousness OF. You have been conscious OF every experience that makes up your life. Without consciousness there could not have been any experience that might have been noted.

So here we are at the station, which is consciousness — the sphere where experience is happening.

Consciousness through this interface seemingly comes in contact with our world. By becoming conscious of thoughts a mental experience is formed that takes your attention and puts it into a realm of mind that no one else can go to: YOUR own realm of mind. **Your own little What's Not Happening**.

Rarely is your What's Not Happening matching someone else's What's Not Happening. Communication here is very, very difficult, since people are talking about What's Not Happening. Their condition last week, or what they hope will happen. Their whole state of being isn't being; it's a mental state of was-ing and will-ing.

The only true stated communication is being now.

Every train is witnessed by consciousness. Each one came through the station. Trains to Philadelphia, trains to Boston, trains, trains, trains. It doesn't matter their destinations, they're all witnessed by the station. The station is the one stable thing for all the trains.

So you're like a station. You're the interface for this world, for this experience.

Every train with all its feelings and thoughts is noted — but only as it's going through.

Once it's gone through its not the station's business anymore, which is constantly awake to what's happening. The station is awake to the mental experience of What's Not Happening, but it doesn't get on any train that goes through the station. It cannot give up its station-hood to become a passenger on the train.

It witnesses all the acts of you as a long-lasting independent separate entity which is just a mental process called selfing, getting on trains and getting off trains, having great expectations and great disappointments, and so on and so forth. All this activity of selfing is being witnessed by the station. The station would no longer be the station if it got on the train. It would become a passenger.

Our state as the station, of being a witness, has seemingly been forgotten. This mind has forgotten its own nature and has become identified with the projection of a mental process that I call selfing because it's a verb, not a noun. It's not real. It only seems real by its sense of being continual.

This sense of being a noun is that of being a passenger. The passenger is going to be totally affected by what train he gets on, or what train someone else gets on. I should not have gotten on that train.on. Selfing, selfing, selfing.

A lot comes with you when you get on that train. A lot of old ideas, a lot of beliefs; you are a catacomb of conditioning called the idea of being a self. And that gets downloaded on every little trip you take as a passenger. You give the trains all the meaning they have. **I'll judge the train, that it's to blame that I didn't get where I wanted to go.**

Everyone said it would get me where I'm going! Something must be deeply wrong with the train — or else with me.

I can try to figure out which trains are the good ones, practice deciphering the hieroglyphics on the side of the trains so I can ascertain which ones might take me to heaven or to hell. That activity is hellish, so obsessed with trying to figure things out. There's no lightness in that.

Maybe I go looking for the Schedule of All Schedules! Maybe a really old one from a cave in the Himalayas that will tell me about all the trains, when they come in and where they go. Even so I'll still be a passenger, without a sense of the true quality of my nature, which is awareness, the station.

Being at the station is like a long pause. An eternal moment. There is no time in a pause.

Your mind, when introduced to what's obvious, has the ability to be convinced by its own recognition that this place is totally crazy and contrived, that it's a dream. An active realization takes place. Because it's so easy to see what's not happening for what it is – What's Not Happening!

So entertain a pause. You can live in that pause. That's the station. It is a recognition of what's obvious, here in the moment. **The simple recognition that your mental experience is truly not happening on the level you think it is. Its reality is only seemingly so. That's your release. Your relief.**

A mind identified as a wave is in denial of the ocean. It's that simple.

All there is, is consciousness. **All you are is THAT. That space in which everything appears, moment by moment streaming through.**

But our minds become identified with appearances. The mind has become identified as the body. We're like a bunch of waves looking at the other waves, totally consumed in a wave world of our own interpretation, when all there is is ocean.

"That wave's faster than I am. That wave is getting to the shore before me. I want to pick up the shells. I don't want to break in Stinson Beach, I want to break in Hawaii."

There is a seeing that is available at all times. No matter what your head is telling you about what's looking, **underneath all that is pure seeing.** All the time. Every moment. Seeing is not defined by your idea of what looking is, with all the opinions, pontificating, judgments and critiques of how you're doing and not doing.

As Buddha said: When you feel, feel. When you taste, taste. When you touch, touch. When you smile, smile. When you think, think. This is conscious contact.

The conditioned head acknowledges the conscious contact, consciousness moving through the body, then the head claims it: Paul is seeing; Paul is hearing. Paul tastes that burrito. The object has claimed the movement of subjectivity through it and now claims the expression of subjectivity as "mine."
This selfing is such a small mental process. Its whole claim to fame is being a body. From this appearance of the body it produces the effect of being a self. Like an intoxicant. Everything it entertains is entertained as the self, which limits what it can entertain. Everything is perceived as to how it pertains to me. In the process there is a denial of THAT — the ocean — though all that is, is that.

You cannot entertain the truth as the self because you cannot make the truth an object. It's the subject of all subjects. If you want to be a self it has to be an object to you; and that's why you'll never know the truth.

Everywhere cannot be recognized by a special somewhere. It's impossible. It's the recognition that you're not this, the body, that affords you the vision of seeing from everywhere. Things that were confusing get very clear.

"You" become irrelevant. Hallelujah.

As a wave there is concern about where you'll break. But as the ocean? Obviously not. Appearances change but the quality of ocean remains. Just a movement of mind called selfing. Appearing to be a self. When in fact nothing has changed.

The mind requires relevance. Always doing and having, to attain value for itself. When you were a kid you didn't need to accrue value; it's when you grew into selfing that you decided you had to make yourself into something.

Did you think that way when you were three years old? Were you having these incredible convoluted moments and concerns? "I have no value." No. You were too busy playing, running around, immediate and spontaneous. The narration had not begun. The introspection had not yet begun. This whole partitioning of everywhere into all these special somewhere segments had not begun. The gated community of the Special Somewhere that negates the Everywhere had not yet been built.

Qualities of that unadorned life were wonder and awe, which now seem infrequent for most adults.

So let's say you find out the trouble is self. Do you sign up for the two-year course, "How to get over the obsession with self"? Wouldn't that be obsession with self? Self can't get out of self. How could a product of a mental process ever leave the mental process? How could a wave ever leave the ocean? It's meant to arise and to depart. The question is, could you ever be a self? If you are not in, there is no need to get out.

And all the fears that accompany that nature of coming and inevitably going are deeply embedded in that condition, the fear of dying, because your wave will be over then. How many waves have broken out in the ocean? Billions and billions of them. Has the ocean ceased to be? No. You want fear to be removed? Remove what thinks it has the fear! How you remove it is to realize it was never there to begin with. What works for me is to realize I'm not a self. It gets me out of what I could never be in. Released from the need to seek a way out of it.

It's really incredible when you parachute into this moment. Just drop in and you're totally here.

No idea of any place being better than here, or reflecting that once there was ever a greater here. Dismissed from the mental interpretation. What is obvious is obvious. No more trying to get out of what we can't be in, or get into what we can't be out of.

Everyone here thinks they are an individual wave in the ocean. And of course we have our wave worries. "Who's going to beat me to shore. I've got a lot of kelp in me, how did I get that? Did anyone see me from the beach? Am I a cresting wave or a droopy wave?"

Attention and interest totally consumed with wave qualities.

All those ideas of being a wave are produced by the mental process. The mental process is telling you how to be a wave. Re-presenting what it's like to be a wave. What it was like to be a past wave. Definitely, what it's like to be a future wave. All the while there is forgetfulness of the essence of every wave, which is the ocean.

Coming to a meeting as waves to discuss the topic of the ocean is in a deep sense hilarious. **Because all you need to do – is nothing. All the doing is an activity of being a wave.** The wave trying to grasp the essence of the ocean is only reaffirming its wave-ness. Defining the ocean as something I'm separate from, yet want to have an experience of."

Which is self's true security! It will adore the ocean as long as it can do that as a wave. It may consider one wave like a Jesus or Buddha and say, "Oh yes, he or she was the ocean," as long as it's not now; we don't want any live ocean at the moment. Because then one would see through the game of being a wave.

So we're not discussing the qualities and depth of the ocean – only questioning, "Are you a wave?" If you realize you are not a wave – slap! – you're immediately the ocean! Inherently you're not a wave; you're space expressing itself as appearances. You're the ocean expressing itself as a wave.

To another wave you are a wave. That's the way a wave sees another wave. The act of seeing waves as waves is an active denial of the ocean, placing attention on what it's like to be a wave but not what it's like to be the ocean.

As soon as you see with the possibility that, "I may possibly not be that," what may occur is that the truth will ring true and you will drop into what was never left.

There will be a sense of ocean while there is the appearance of a wave. They're not exclusive.

When the wave recognizes it's the ocean that doesn't stop it from appearing as a wave. The wave can continue to be wavelike; but now there is a sense of being the ocean. Allowing the wave to travel lighter. Actually enjoy its waveness. In the presence of the wetness, the immensity of the ocean, all the worries about being a wave become dismissed. **You see the wave is a little bogus presentation.**

Once you recognize the ocean, it doesn't negate the appearance of the wave. We simply recognize it for the appearance it is. The appearance rises and has its little life moving toward the shore and breaks on it. A moment in the ocean. No ocean died; the ocean did not disappear, only an appearance of it did. All appearances are destined o disappear.

What we are is that space in which everything is allowed to appear. And everything that appears has a nature: it's going to disappear. Every wave is going to crest and break.

When I pick up the chair you don't see any remnants of the chair. You may see its effects on other appearances, perhaps marks on the floor, but the space is as though there never had been a chair. It didn't take weeks of practice to realize there was never a chair; it's just immediately as though there was never a chair. The chair is just an appearance in space, like the wave.

People practice for years and have a lot of experiences of the ocean, but always AS a wave. We take ourselves to be this real solid wave and the ocean appears to have a quality we want.

Waving and waving and waving. Seeing only appearances, taking this wave to be real. Living on the surface of the ocean as though there were only what was appearing there. So concerned with what is going to happen to me — an appearance.

It's like light on water. Your mind likes to follow that light. It gets engaged with the blips. And while engaged with the light on the surface it doesn't sense the wholeness. A little dance on the infinity of the ocean. The mind is identified with this appearance called Paul. Totally engaged. It's forgotten its nature of being an ocean.

I don't try to show you a picture of the ocean, saying, "Look how big and wonderful it is." **Because every time you're looking at it, you're looking at it from the point of view of being a wave.**

You may decide, "I want to feel the ocean as a wave. I want to become the ocean as a wave. I've been practicing at this temple of oceanness for 20 years."

But the wave is persistently established AS YOU. That's the denial of the qualities of the ocean. You don't see the wave as the deterrent. Not that you can't get the ocean. You ARE the ocean.

What's the dilemma here? With the identification in place that I'm a wave the only thing the ocean can be to me is an experience. The mind wants to have an experience of the ocean, but if push comes to shove it's going to hang on to the idea of being a wave.

I don't care about the beauty of the ocean; I want to question the wave. **If I'm not the wave – boom! I'm the ocean.**

The special somewhere is trying to take on the qualities of Everywhere. You cannot take on the qualities of Everywhere as a special somewhere. You ARE the Everywhere.

For the special somewhere to take on the qualities of the Everywhere is to extract the Everywhere-ness out of it.

We live as though we are the one solid long-lasting thing here.

What's appearing seems so incredibly important. But what's appearing is not incredibly important – not to the space. And if you're truly THAT . . . Ha ha ha ha! To give all of that up for this (thumping the body) – it's like that movie in which Nicholas Cage decides to give up being an angel in order to make it with Meg Ryan. (Probably to get divorced two years later.) What an insane arrogance of appearances!

Like a freakin' angel would give up its angelhood to come here, for that? The appearance thinking it's so much cooler to be an appearance than all of THAT. Give me a freaking break. The Archangel Michael ought to slap some sense into him. "Come on, Bro. You're delusional. You want to appear and disappear?"

The wave can have exquisite suffering. All those crazy ideas that you can entertain when you believe you are separate from the ocean. Believing love has to come from outside; that peace is something you can do and have, that you have to do something to get serenity.

Talk about consumerism! We've become consumers ever since we became identified as this head. Seeking constantly. Consuming experiences. Believing the more experiences we have the more we'll have of life. But experiences come and go. They are an appearance to an appearance.

And if we keep on identifying with what we're not? It's exhausting being separate. Do you know how much work your mind has to do to be a wave? It's got to be on it all day long.

All day meanwhile the wetness of the ocean is seeping through its little concept of being a wave.

When the truth comes through, not to you but through you, it's set down as a "spiritual experience." A pause. Moment of respite. "Oh, what did I do for that to happen? I'll go over what I did that feels so good."

You didn't do anything! Your true nature seeped through, that's all.

Wetness becomes a commodity that dryness tries to find. Or sell. Or privatize. When it is our inherent nature to be wet! As your nature continues to seep through, the wave will dream itself out of the dream of being a wave and the ocean-ness will be more and more obvious. There will be more wetness in it.

There is a subservience to the mental realm. The mind is re-presenting conscious contact as you being the one that's conscious, which is causing a total experience of unconsciousness. Totally unconscious to the fact of ocean.

All day, totally in the appearance of being a wave. The life of a wave re-presented constantly. "I could have been bigger, I should have been smaller." It goes on and on. Your interest is absorbed in it. Unbelievable. All the attention thrown into "me." And what a return!

What do you need to do about it? Absolutely nothing. Just become awake to it.

It's really just getting disarmed in a sense, all your little mechanisms. Putting down the grasping. Noticing what's obvious. It's consciousness. Seeing.

Because the mind says, "I'm seeing," that doesn't mean it's true. Just a mental process claiming the seeing. The little mind can claim the big mind. The big mind is just seeing. Always available at all times. No matter how much clinging, how much claiming you do, the one moment it's entertained not to be you, it all stops.

.

You don't leave the ocean of being, become a noun, and have a different experience of life, as island life.

There is no island! There is only being.

Being is an uninterrupted verb. There is no island of noun to climb up on. There is only Being, conscious contact, present action in progress: A VERB. But the head has made a NOUN of it, called ME.

It works like this: There is an experience — conscious contact. Then the mind claims to be the one who HAD the experience — wrapping all the little stories together into a big story of being a SELF that claims those stories to imply its reality.

This occurs because of identification AS the body. I seem to be looking through this body, so I take it as A BODY THAT IS LOOKING. The body is fitted with the idea of being "me."

Now that conscious contact has been hijacked, I am informed every moment that I am a self WHO IS IN conscious contact (rather than conscious contact itself).

The counter evidence of this idea is available at all times through the conscious contact itself. As Buddha said, when seeing, see; when hearing hear.

There's a neuroscientist I heard speak once. He said there is an 'experiential self' and a 'remembering self.'

Now to me there is no 'self'; so I refer to an 'experiential mode' and a 'remembering mode.' What is well-being and happiness for one mode is not for the other. Here's the difference:

The **remembering mode** is about what I've done and what I have, like the big game hunter with antlers over the mantle. I'm happy because I've done this and done that. In this remembering mode there is on-going judging and comparison to see how good or bad one's doing.

But the **experiential mode** doesn't find happiness in the resume or the goals it's attained. This mode is pure Being. Conscious contact. Its joy in life is in the process rather than the destination. The experiential doesn't care about judging and comparing; it doesn't have time for any of that because there's no time for getting out of the experience and becoming an observer of it! There is in fact no time.

When the remembering mind takes over and it's totalling up to see how good and bad you are, it's totally insane. It has its own agenda. You may think it's working for you, but you're actually working for it. It's using your life to interpret life based on its own views. Its desire to be right is incredibly powerful, as is its desire to be special. Nor does it care "how" its special: A 10-year prison sentence can be just as special to it as buying a house in Pacific Heights.

The main difference in the two: There has to be a sense of being a self for the remembering mode. But there doesn't have to be any sense of self for the experience mode. The mental process uses experience to infer an experiencer. And uses memory to "remember a self."

In my younger years there was no idea of Paul; it wasn't set in concrete yet. When I was playing there was no worry, would I be playing next week. I had no idea of next week. Absolutely none. I wasn't walking around our house thinking my room was too small or that my mother was fat.

A light way to travel, yes? Wonder, awe, spontaneity. Then we outgrow it.

Actually, we grow into something else which excludes that. What is it that we grow into? A REMEMBRANCE of a life. There's judgment, good and bad; should've done this and that. There is a separation from the very EXPERIENCE of living into the OBSERVANCE of living.

What's observing is not you. What's observing is **the conditioning**. You're looking through your mother's eyes, your grandmother's eyes, a teacher's eyes, your friends' eyes; not so much experiencing as thinking about the experiences afterwards. What does it mean? **The mind gets into the story.**

You're never out of life. **But you separate yourself out**, so that there is an event going on but you think it is happening TO YOU. That instead of proceeding THROUGH an event it's happening TO you. Meanings are being inserted into life based on WHAT thinks it's living it.

Enslaved to thoughts?

The mind is obsessed with the idea of being a self. And it doesn't recognize: That's the dilemma.

Your attention orbits around the **Planet of Self.** The self provides **the gravitational pull to all the thoughts, making them about YOU.**

If you realized they weren't about the REAL you, they could simply come and go. Your attention would be freed up from the slavery of selfing and would attend to the conscious contact: A recognition of life in and of itself. You'd be travelling lighter — not by any procedures or practice but simply by recognition of what is not so.

The reason I'm hooked on the narrative in my head is because I think it's about me. By freeing up some of the attention from the selfing there is awareness of the conscious contact; then the enslavement is over. Once you recognize you're not the self you will lose interest in all its activities. Simply by entertaining that the selfing is not "you."

You'll lose interest in obsessing with the thoughts, making up stories about the feelings you're having or not having. The attention that's glued to the screen of selfing will be released; it will be available to the conscious contact — each moment's experience. A sense of awareness will grow. That awareness is what we are.

Most of your attention goes to what's NOT happening (the past and future) instead of what IS happening.

When that devotional practice of selfing is dismissed you can attend to what IS happening: The conscious state of what you are — conscious contact. You'll be aware of existing. The I am.

When that "I am" is in place you can have an immunity to all the "I am nots." Simple as that! Just an entertaining of the I am gives you recognition of what "is." The I am becomes obvious through recognizing what you're not.

You think living is about something that has happened, or something that may happen. You think living is about having expectations, **withholding yourself from this moment in favor of a mythical moment that will be better than this moment, because it seems like there's nothing happening in this moment**. From what point of view? From the point of view of the self as a noun! What else could this be called but slavery?

Life is a verb — appearing every moment new. Always happening. Otherwise, it would be called "was-ing." or "will-be-ing." Selfing works wonders with this; you could "was" yourself into a great mythical past or "will-be" yourself into a hopeful (or fearful!) mythical future. But all of nothing's happening. This mental process is an impotent waving of an imaginary wand.

In selfing life is happening TO you.

Self has become such a strong reference point that everything that is happening is now happening TO you.

That's a huge interpretation, and when you interpret life you miss it. It's impossible not to. You cannot corral a verb. You just go along with it.

You don't have to CHANGE the fact that you're living totally in interpretation. Attend to the awareness; and that awareness will stop your attention from giving up to selfing. **That whole production will move to the background; and the background, which is the awareness, will move to the foreground.** The emphasis will shift. And you'll travel lighter.

Just entertain the idea you're not the self you think you are.

All the body-brain processes have been used by the mental process called selfing to facilitate the bondage of self (being a body). When you see you are not that which is being inferred and implied, you will lose interest in self. Thoughts will not be held as your thoughts; feelings will not be held as your feelings.

A thought is just a thought; but it changes dramatically when it becomes MY thought.

The interpretation of the thought as being mine is slapped on it. Now the thought, whose nature it is to come and go, doesn't go by so quickly anymore.

A thought comes into awareness. You hear the thought. But how you hear it is, "I'm the thinker of it." The thought becomes observed as being mine. The act of identification. My thought.

You own the thought; the thought owns you. You are the haver of the feeling; the feeling has you.

The MY connects it with the file system called Paul. Paul has a lot of files about life related to Paul. **As soon as the thought becomes identified as MY thought the file system gets opened**, pulling up old ideas and downloading them into the thought. The binding agent isn't the thought; your claiming it is the binding agent.

Now you're bound to that thought; and instead of going on its way it's orbiting around you. The Planet of You provides the gravitational pull that keeps the thoughts circling.

If you lose interest in the idea that you are that planet then you will lose interest in the THOUGHTS ABOUT YOU as that planet --- releasing the thoughts from their gravitational orbit so that they can come and go, and they are freed, and so are you.

The self thinks it can know the truth because it plays the subject and makes truth the object. But that's not what's happening. The truth is all there is, and I'm seeing FROM it right now — but not as a Paul; that's a story ABOUT the seeing.

You know FROM the truth.

Self loops everything back to itself in a loop of self reflection. You get absorbed in that because you think it's you.

So now a question, a self inquiry, a good little tool. Try it:

Knock on the door. Ask, "Who am I?"

The head says, "It's me." Ask again. What happens? If you continue to do this, you run into pure awareness.

So there's a stop, a pause, and you get a free sample. It will trick the selfing into submission for a second perhaps, and there will be a pause in the selfing.

Because selfing is a verb it can be stopped; you can throw a wrench into it.

One part of your energy is always looking out, attending to things. Another part of your energy is going back into self. Referring all the contact back to ME, saying I am what is in contact, I.

So we're going to ask who am I. The selfing, busily being the I, goes, "I heard the door," and turns to it. And because it's not the self, but the awareness, awareness meets the awareness. Bingo. There's the freedom from the bondage of self.

When you no longer pontificate about what's happening, then you are in conscious contact, where the rubber meets the road. There is life, happening. I don't know what happened yesterday, and I don't care; the context of this day was enough. There was one thing that was always going on, which was the verbing of it. Always the sense of being. The sense of movement. Of presence. The generator of life humming in the background.

We might say, awareness is you; but that's stretching it. There's just awareness. This whole act of sensing the being of it is the joy.

Someone will say, maybe you can help me get on to that awareness thing, maybe I'll feel better.

The lie is that you can ever be "off" the awareness. Consciousness is a constant state. It doesn't have to get ready. It doesn't take a vacation and come back. It's always on. No entrance point, no exit point. You're on the ride, there's no getting off.

Feel the energy. Be the verb. **We're trying to signal you, through the wall of the noun that you're really a verb.** That's all that's happening. Trying to tickle the verb through this shell of a noun.

Do you want to be the thing that can be aware half the time, or do you want to be the awareness?

You can't serve two masters at the same time. Serving the one master frees you up to travel lighter. Serving the other master wants to exclude you by HAVING you, as a noun.

You're being taken over by the parasite. Of course you want relief! The stories aren't you; but if you decide to believe they are your attention can be drawn into them. And you're stuck.

The mind feels very safe in the idea you MIGHT be conscious one day.

"When I do such and such then I, as the mind, will allow myself to feel how conscious I am." But never now; it's always put off. Because being conscious, NOW, would be the end of self.

Self doesn't exist. Only the process of living, the verb, exists.

There is selfing, but there is no self. Selfing is not a problem; what is the problem is the illusion of being a self. Selfing will keep happening. The real solution is to recognize you're not the self or the selfing; then all the perceptions of illusion can keep appearing and making an illusion – which you're not falling for anymore! For without you there is no illusion. Illusions must be entertained: without the entertainer there is no illusion.

Like Jesus said, "You are the light of this world," but you've put a basket over your light. The basket is the idea of being a self.

Selfing says, I want to be the awareness.

No you frickin' don't. You don't want to be free. You just want to have a better self. Want everything to get better just as you are.

The basic fact of living is the awareness of it. There is only consciousness.

When we forget that we ARE conscious contact there's trouble, because life is no longer experienced as what is simply happening, but as what is happening TO ME.

Trying to get a solution? To what? To get out of self? Sounds like a natural response to a situation that's unbearable. But the response is part and parcel of the bigger problem, called self-centeredness. It's called duality. Your trying to get out of it is being in it. How can we escape from an imaginary place?

All the thoughts that are happening in your head are a product of the system of self centeredness.

Whatever has happened in your life, self takes advantage of it. Polishes it, cherishes it, makes it the basis of its story. No way it's going to let loose of it. It receives whatever your life comes in contact with and takes advantage of it.

You realize finally there is no need to be liberated. All that needs to be liberated is you, from the idea of being a noun.

There is an event going on, you think it is happening to you as a self. You don't see yourself as proceeding THROUGH an event, but as an event that's happening TO you.

When you think life is happening TO you, thousands of files download. This system of self centeredness gives meaning to life through you. You see the meaning as though it's real and solid and outside of yourself. There is life. Then it becomes my life. My self. Makng this huge movie about me.

I attempted to get better through spiritual practices.

I was in that marketplace quite a while. I figured that was the only place to find value in life, those practices. Always seeking for 10 years or so, but formulated in self-centeredness. All to be a BETTER SELF: "I as Paul am going to do something and have something for Paul to be better."

That's the only way I could think; I didn't know any better. I couldn't think outside the box, because if you THINK you're still in the box. All the thinking I could entertain was defined by self-centeredness.

Then I met someone who talked about this position of the pointless point. I entertained the possibility. I got the flavor of it, I sensed it. Once I entertained it, it became the last answer for me. Maybe I'll get a new answer, but I haven't for years.

Now Paul doesn't have to be so busy with doing and having, getting better and worse. It's produced good things through this life.

We are overwhelming what's happening with what's not happening. It's amazing if you turn on to entertaining something that is true, what it can produce. In self-centeredness there is only a very limited range of possibility. It's the same old same old. You've been into every nook and cranny already.

If you apply a solution to an imaginary problem (self) what can you expect?

A lot of something's going to happen, but it's not going to be what you thought. If you apply a solution to an imaginary problem what you're doing is verifying the reality of the problem. You are reality lending itself to what the mind takes itself to be so.

What solution that you think you've found has lasted? None. How can a solution work on an imaginary problem? The true solution is recognizing its imaginary; that's the quickest way out. To realize you're not in it.

You lose total interest finally in being "liberated," because you realize there is no need to be liberated. All that needs to be liberated is your freedom from the idea of being a noun, from what you're not. That's it; that's as far as liberation needs to go.

That's the whole solution. The recognition that I was never in what I thought I was in, and I was trying so hard to get out of it. I stopped; I was out of it by not trying to be out of it.

You see what you're not from what you are. But you cannot see what you are from what you're not. It's impossible.

That's why you think you're missing it; because you want to see "what is" from a special somewhere, which causes you to be blind to everywhere.

The head is adamant about being a special somewhere. Recognizing everywhere would erase the belief in being a special somewhere. Just like that! So it's willing to accommodate an IDEA of everywhere while remaining a special somewhere.

Let's say I'm desiring to have a spiritual experience. A little taste of everywhere. But that's like having a fish deciding to pour a glass of water on itself to experience being wet. "Oh, now I'm wet." It's already totally immersed in water! For it to want to experience being wet it has to believe it's dry.

It's not about getting wet; it's about recognizing what's telling you you're dry!

Seeking began in America in a big way about 40 years ago. I'm going to do and have myself into a spiritual condition in the hope of acquiring some advantage, AS ME.

For a lot of people it has failed to deliver.

We become identified with the body, which is a perfect demonstration of a dualistic construct. Then we decide we want to entertain singularity — but AS the body. How could duality ever entertain singularity?

The object takes itself to be the subject. Then the true subject (consciousness itself) becomes an object to it.

If you, as a dualistic construct, take yourself to be the subject --- then the truth becomes an object to you.

As the truth, pure subjectivity, moves through the apparatus of the body the apparatus takes itself to be the subject by recognizing the movement of subjectivity. "I'm the one that's conscious. Me. I'm the thinker, I am the doer, I am the haver."

When this happens true enlightenment, love, and so on, have to be made into an object, since now you're the subject. **Once you've made the truth, your true nature, into an object to you – you'll never find it.**

When the body-orientation becomes the subject, **I forget the true subject and am looking for it out here in practices that may lead to "enlightenment"** and such.

It's cast in the form of a physical journey: I'm going to purify myself; walk 1000 miles; reach the spiritual oasis of Nirvana, and so on.

It's failed miserably!

Because what's seeing has been projected outside into something the looker, me, can find. The apparatus is not recognizing the pure subjectivity looking through it.

As Buddha said: when you feel, feel. When you taste, taste. When you touch, touch. When you smile, smile. When you think, think.

Self. It's whole claim to fame is being a body. This body. This appearance. It produces the effect of being a self. Like an intoxicant. It can only entertain peace and surrender as a self; and that's not peace and surrender. Everything it entertains is entertained as the self, which limits what it can entertain.

Again: You cannot entertain the truth as the self because you cannot make the truth an object. It's the subject of all subjects. You make it an object to you; and that's why you'll never know the truth. Because you have to cast it as an object with yourself as the subject.

We are saddled with the proscribed way of looking called self-centeredness. Everything is perceived as to how it pertains to me.

The thing to do is to turn the light on it to see that all there is, is subject; there is no object called me as a subject.

There's just subjectivity. That's the truth.

Then enlightenment and all these goals become non-goals, because you realize there is nothing to seek. I am that which I've been looking for. Ding!

Who's the meditator?

Around 1998 I was looking for yet another form of meditation. Looking for some turbo-charged kundalini meditation because I'd already been through Vipassana and Zen and various others.

The person I went to see just said a simple thing to me: "Why not just ask, 'Who's the meditator?' Instead of looking for another technique or mediation, instead of shopping for the next spiritual thing?"

Now this was monumental to me.

Blue belts, black belts. The self loves belts signifying that it's gotten to a certain level.

Any process is manna from heaven to the selfing. It gets to have something to do. All these movements of selfing, constantly, constantly.

If I'm talking with someone who's really into some spiritual approach I want to ask:

But what do you do about that mental paradigm of the doing and having? There is a Zen treatise called "Faith Mind," in which the author warns us, "You cannot use activity to produce stillness. That would be activity."

Let's say you are doing and having in a way the mind thinks is noble. Then it is ripe for the identification as a self, as the doer. A fertile field for the conditional mind. An archetypical idea you have of something that is noble, God or whatever – that's the biggest minefield [mind field?] of them all. Every time you're involved with it there will be the reflection of being a doer. It's difficult to see through; and it becomes more sublime the more "noble" the path is.

There is an overriding mental modality. The more meaning the thing you're doing gets, the more glue is being applied through the doing. If you think it's really important what you're doing and having, the glue of being the doer of that is like crazy glue.

So I did that. There seemed nobility in doing all that; but all the while the mind was feasting. Just making a new self, turning it into a spiritual self. Hours of sitting, going to Thailand, going to India, it was writing up a great new story. Because the old addict story was over, it had run its course, milked that dead cow for years. Now becoming a spiritual giant, whew! Milking that for all it's worth.

The mind gives meaning to things.

Another identity was setting up. The mind had investment in it. Was protecting and promoting it. All the while thinking it was escaping the plight of humanity; but there was more bullshit than ever.

It's the same mental game. Forming an identity, unbelievably. With the idea that you're getting out of the mortal coil.

In fact, it's the binding agent. What you call your escape is actually the prison. Every escape your mind is looking for is actually the act of being imprisoned. Imprisoned to that mind, that selfing, because you're identified with what that selfing reflects: A self.

The ordinary is the greatest door. It's the one you walk through and don't give much meaning to. Something can shift. You can come out of self. Recognize the availability of presence.

We're not giving much meaning to all that is, though it is happening all the time. We're giving tons of meaning to appearances that are going to come and go. But we don't give any meaning to what is always so. That's the beauty of it, it's so ordinary and so contextual that we miss it.

If something is shiny to the mind it will be used as a mirror to the self. This message you're hearing today has no shine to it; you get nothing. You're getting nothing. **It disarms all of the importance the mind likes to have**. It's the greatest thing to receive – nothing. Everything else will be used by mind. But this "nothing," the mind has no idea what to do with it. Though nothing is the gift that keeps on giving. People keep getting more and more something, and it seems always to add up to nothing; why not start there?

The gravity story.

You walk into a café on any given day, you'll not hear anyone complaining about gravity. When they come back from a hard hike, they'll be blaming the hill that they're exhausted. But was it the hill or was it gravity?

No on is acknowledging the effect of gravity since the body is always under it. The way we would learn about the effects of gravity would be to have an experience of no-gravity.

It's like a fish in the water. It recognizes what appears in the water, clams, fish, but never recognizes what it's in. Only recognizes the meaning of water when it's out and flopping on the deck.

So you know the problem from the solution. From the problem there is a strong need for a solution. From the solution there is no real problem.

The mind is like a crazy weatherman. Predicting storms every day.

Telling you even if it's sunny you can't enjoy it because a big storm's coming. Is that peace? A short bit of peace that precedes a longer term of storm? Is that what peace is?

Peace is prior to that. Peace is not established by circumstances and situations.

The root of the dilemma is an identification with a mental image called self. The mind presents you as a body. Then a lot of mental states and processes are taken to be private states and processes — as being yours – and they're not. Just produced by the mind.

You live in a realm of time, a mental realm. The sense of being a long-lasting independent separate entity is generated by the apparatus. It's a feeling combined with a thought. The body's language is feelings; the mind's language is thinking.

Sensations of the body are hijacked by the mental process which spins out a story of feelings about you. About what was you and what is going to be you. Then the thoughts reinforce that. Obsessing over self all day.

Self has to conjure up a sense of reality out of essentially nothing. Because there is no reality to it. The show is based upon the true platform of reality which is conscious contact.

The seeing, tasting, and touching needs to happen through a body. Consciousness could not have a contact with this place except through a body. It has to go through certain doors. The door of vision, of taste, etc. Consciousness enlivens the body in order to facilitate the experience.

Consciousness is going through the doors of the senses and meeting itself here. The mental process then claims it: I am the one seeing, doing, etc. It's my body.

Conditional mind is the puppet theater. Claiming the demonstration of being here, the conscious contact, seeing, feeling, tasting, touching. Making it into "my seeing" and "my touching."

A thought is just a thought until it becomes your thought. How does it become your thought? There's a claiming of it. A mental process. Does that imply there is a you claiming that? No. Only to you does that imply that. Only to the you that it's made up.

It's not a matter of knowing the truth or not knowing the truth. There is no need to know the truth. None whatsoever. You are THAT! Know the false and be the truth.

The game has nothing to do with you. You're like a narrator of the game.

You cannot call the game off. The mind is narrating it with a sense of you being a player.

You already know what the game is like when you're identified as the body. Now you might see how it goes when you're not.

I don't want self-knowledge. I want knowledge that will lead me to the freedom from self.

You'll see the solution by the problem's absence. When that narration is dismissed you realize, "That's what I was suffering from!"

The narration about the journey is the heaviness.

If there is a sense of what's happening NOW you won't be living in a house built upon the past.

Once it gets erased on the blueprint level you're living outdoors in a sense. Free ranging. No longer in a little conceptual tenement with the hallway of the past decorated with all your secrets and reasons why you're not happy now. All the hopes of how you'll be saved. The quality you can never have in that mental tenement.

There is an immunity to all that advertising being presented. The greatest immunity is being here, the sense of conscious contact.

You can't see it, what you're worried about, can you? Can't taste it, can't touch it. You think you're feeling it and you're thinking of it, but you can't see it, feel it, smell it. For all intents and purposes it's not happening.

The interest and attention follow the trail of crumbs to "what's not happening," attentive to a made-up anxiety. Then interest and attention download it into the apparatus, which is your vehicle of experience, for the experience of "what's not happening." Pure unadulterated mental anxiety.

If you went to a place that wasn't happening, could you bring back a product from there? No? Sure you can. If you believe in what's not happening you will bring back mental anxiety and fear, and lots more. What a terrible trip!

Why so open to those products? Why are you willing to take rotten fruit every day? You're like a garage the truck backs up and dumps into. Then you deal with the smell and the rottenness of it. And the mind makes up a story about you, makes it right for it to be unbearable, so that at least you're right while it's unbearable. It was them! If they hadn't done this and that I'd be okay.

Amazing isn't it? Isn't it enough just to live a day here? Why so necessary to have hundreds of days in the future and hundreds of days in the past, to harvest those fields with mental crops? To download them to your little market every day. You have to travel with all that.

And when you do? You download it on others don't you? Call them up and say how disappointed you are in what's not happening. Then they dump their what's not happening on you. Like a fish market with 10-day-old fish.

I'm so flipped out about next Friday. But it's not happening. Oh! But I'm still flipped out about next Wednesday. But that's not happening.

We're here, but to all intents and purposes we live as though we are not here. Living in the mental realm of what's not happening. We join in, have parties with each other, giant phone bills.

So go to the root of what's truly not happening: A self. A long-lasting independent separate entity is what's not happening. To realize that is freedom.

All the intrinsic contracts you have with what's not happening are based on "you" as the original what's not happening. **If you break the contract you'll have immunity.** A position of neutrality to the past and future. Not indifference, but neutrality.

Then what's not happening no longer draws your interest and attention from what's seeing. All your interest and attention that's been invested in what's not happening is brought back to conscious contact, living, now, creating lots of dividends. The same attention to that which is driving us crazy is now enriching our day.

You're traveling lighter. A certainty arises. Your attention now knows its source, which is not self. You are a conveyor of interest and attention, which is resting in its source of awareness and is no longer fooled by the misidentification. It has plenty of interest and attention to attend to the demands and requests and invitations of the day without losing the sense of its real nature. Not going to self and getting caught in that black hole.

Very few people give much attention to nothingness. They think it has no value. Though nothingness is the freedom from appearances.

Here's the message: Consciousness — that's all there is.

You're conscious; all there is is consciousness; you're conscious; all there is is consciousness; you're conscious; all there is is consciousness. Ding!

"I'm conscious." No, all there is is consciousness. "I'm conscious." No, all there is is consciousness. "I'm conscious." No, all there is is consciousness. Ding! If all there is is consciousness, there's no room for a "me."

Be conscious. That's it. That's the message.

All your dilemmas are based on being couscious as a "me." You're not that. So there's your solution.

"But I don't want that solution." Fine.

"Let's discuss it." No. It's not a point of debate, it's an invitation. If you find value in it great. Otherwise keep shopping. You're going to be constantly seeking some relief from the "me" you think you are.

The "me" is what's broadcasting all your "suffering." That's where it all emanates from. You want to get relief while you hold on to that? You'll be busy. Whatever relief you apply to it will run out and you'll need to go look for more. The "me" is the Petrie dish where all the suffering is given life and sustenance.

Life becomes a form of seeking. For what? To get relief FOR the "me." Why not get relief FROM the "me"?

"Then what am I?" You're consciousness. The living expression of you is consciousness; it has nothing to do with the entity you've taken yourself to be.

"I, Paul, am what is conscious." Is it? Take a look. **The idea of the "I" is that it's the doer of life.** When you realize you're not the doer of life, whose life is it anyway? It was never yours to begin with.

The apprehension of this message is instantaneous. The entertaining of it up here (in the head) can be arduous, because you keep trying to entertain it as something that you're not. When the mind gets the smell of what's happening here it will lose interest, because it wants to get ahead, look like its getting "better."

"How could I be spiritual unless I do something to accrue spiritual value?" Which is playing God again

How can something that's already fine, and SO, get better? An impossibility. That doesn't give much room for a star in the movie, does it? The mind would rather not be okay, then get better; that makes for quite a production. "I was down; now I've become . . ."

What happens when there's a bad critic's report?

The head is playing God. Always trying to write its relevance into the story.

Every second of every day. Critiquing you along some scale it's made up. This or that condition. Being liked or not liked. Watching the graphs.

Saint Francis said, "What's looking is what you're looking for."

What disqualifies you from the recognition of what's looking? The head! Doesn't it? Saying looking has to be a certain way.

If the "you" had an option concerning it, it would not be an "optionless state." And it is an optionless state.

If God is everywhere, why aren't you and I bumping into God? Because God is everywhere, and we've made ourselves into a special somewhere. What is that but playing God?

When the head is playing God you are still THAT but you're not BEING it. Giving all your godlike potential to the mental process crowned with the idea of being a self, which channels all the meaning to the small box of interpretation called self-centeredness. The Light of All Lights gets filtered through that and creates this bleak little experience you've been having.

Seeing comes through the apparatus that is identified as the seer, and becomes blind to the seeing by adopting a form of looking called self-centeredness.

Seeing is a verb, happening all the time with no break. It can't be started or stopped; it's an optionless state.

In the seeking there is the sense of being the seek-er. It can identify self as the seeker. If the seeking would stop, there would be finding. Ding! The you that is looking-for is actually the seeing.

As Ramana Maharshi says, "To know God is to be God."

You have the ability to be CONSCIOUS OF. So you can be conscious of your own nature, which is consciousness, or awareness. You are THAT.

You're out on Highway 101, feeling the anxiety of next Friday at work. You've become a time traveler! Your attention is captured by the thoughts. Experiencing the effects now.

WHAT'S NOT HAPPENING overwhelms what IS happening. Now if that's not playing God, what is? Going to a mythical non-happening to download an experiential product — now that's a God! It's going to smite you, Bro! Two places at once. **The body is going to react to whatever is happening in the mind.**

In seeing what you're not, that's the act of being what you are.

The head is a dualistic apparatus. Defined by split mind. Good, bad. Love, hate. Connected, not connected. But consciousness takes out that whole parlor trick.

When you wake up feeling conscious, your first reaction is to think, what did I do to bring this about? What did I do this week, that I'm feeling so conscious? And it's all about you, isn't it? All predicated on you. That's playing God.

Contrarywise, what did I not do, to not feel conscious? Didn't meditate, didn't say my prayers. But your condition is prior to your determining anything. All there is is consciousness. All there is is seeing behind every pair of glasses.

The mind has a difficult time recognizing what is always so. This presence is always so, that's why it seems that it's not so at all. Because of its quality, it's always so. The conditioned mind cannot recognize what's always so.

The fish in the water. Does the fish know it's wet? Not until it's pulled out of the water onto the deck and it's flapping around.

At the café today, did you hear anyone complaining about the effects of gravity? No. Though you're experiencing it every moment of every day. It's always there.

Jesus says, "If the eye is single, the body will be full of light." When you're aware that all there is is consciousness, you're no longer defined by the appearances (duality).

The self-centered mind is playing God. Taking this undifferentiated light and making it into an object. "I can be close to light; I can be far from light."

Who's going to define it? Me. I would say that's playing God.

The mind wants to be relevant. "How can this have anything to do with me?"

Actually it doesn't. "Well let's move on then. Go practice something. Some spiritual practice. I don't like this, I have nothing to do with it, why would I like that? There's no room for me in there at all."

The mind wants to say, "What's looking is based on whether you've been very good," or, "You can't be looking if you've been really bad; so that you have to get busy and purify yourself so that someday . . ."

But who is going to inform you of it? You can hear it from a master, but you'll still be the one to interpret it. You'll find someone to tell you you've got a way to go. It gets overridden by what you think.

Suppose the Dalai Lama says, "It's okay just as it is, as it was, and as it will be. Now go, my sister, and be well." You still don't take it to heart. It gets spun by the head into, "He told me to keep practicing."

That's why all authorities fail you; because you're still the final authority. You'll still be passing judgement on the judgement they pass.

"You're okay." The next step is you'll become un-okay, it won't last.

How long do you have the ability to enjoy peace of mind? You're looking for approval from the head, that will never give it. It can be convinced and un-convinced, just like that.

Simply realize it's not you. When your nature becomes an optionless state, it will stabilize. You'll have an assurance in it, because it's not based on your vote of it's being so or not so. It's so. And that "so" will override your vote of its being so or not so. Always on. Not deviating. So, so, so, so.

Then you get convinced. You have an unspoken yes.

That's when the head presents, "Well, I think I'm going to sign off on your journey now, Paul, I admit you're right, there is only Truth."

And the response to the head: "Hey, too late Bro, the boat left a long time ago and you're still on that shore. Make your little sand castles, bye bye."

It wants to assert itself as an active partner of the light. Wiggle in and make a mark, I was here, I had a part in it. No, it didn't.

So rule 62, don't take yourself so seriously. (From Recovery / AA.)

Aren't you bored of it yet? Can you imagine someone talking to you the way your head talks to you? You'd have left that person in freakin' five minutes. If I knew that person was coming over I'd be out the back door.

Wanting to represent what never really happened over and over again: If I'd not been drinking that night, if I'd not gotten in my car and gone to that bar, and not walked across the street and been hit by that car, I'd be running eight miles, I'd be on the Riviera, instead my whole career was ruined by being run over .

Don't you see, the mind has to make important what isn't happening.

"I'd really be great if I had that." It's playing with us like taffy, pulled this way and that. You can be taken over by the most intense parasite and be claiming to your death bed it was you. Unbelievable.

To see that state as a foreign installment is the only way to be free of it. If you can entertain the little flame that says "I can be free of it," you can travel as if you are free of it. With a new outlook. There's a psychic shift.

Will the dream cease to be if it's recognized as a dream? The dream will continue, only you will no longer be recognized as the dreamt object. There is a more continual resting in the dreaming than in the dream object.

You're going to dream yourself out of the dream; and as you do the dream will become happier. (An idea from the *Course in Miracles.*)

What's not so can appear here in a variety of different ways. But it's just a story. The mind translates it as being relevant to itself. That's what the dream object does here, it translates. Undifferentiated light is coming through and being differentiated. What is that but translation?

A camera translates the light, projected on the screen. You see a movie as the light translates the celluloid. It's the same, what's happening here. Big projector. Light of awareness coming in, being translated by the conditioning of the apparatus, both the collective conditioning and the individual conditioning; and it's being projected out as a movie with you as the star of it.

It's going to be turned into a story no matter what.

The mind is not taking responsibility for being stuck here. It's actually thinking this is imposed on it, that it would do anything to get out of it, but it doesn't want to get out of it really. The whole story of your mind is, you won't get what you want and you may lose what you have.

Wilhelm Reich refers to the emotional plague of a man.
That all of us as a society are in a sort of trap.

A part of the narrative in the trap is that we will do almost anything to get out of the trap; though in fact the mind doesn't really want to go anywhere, it's quite comfortable in the trap.

The solution is available all the time, right where you are. The problem is that you don't want to entertain it. That's the whole point. When someone awake shows up, at first the people like him. They get excited. But the system considers him an incredible threat. The system calls for his death.

"The pure consciousness is available, just like when you're a kid," he tells them. And our whole educational system and societal construct works to kill that consciousness. To kill the imagination. Keeping people in line.

All of us would like to leave the trap if we could, we say; but that's the lie. And if we did? It would be very painful for a few generations while the entire educational system was scrapped and begun again. But once we broke out of it and the consciousness was acknowledged, instead of being diminished, things would go better.

So obviously the United States authorities imprisoned him, Wilhelm Reich, and destroyed his papers. It didn't go over well.

The mind that is practicing all these spiritual practices has no intention of going free. No way. It just makes it feel better about itself. Saying, oh I really would be free if I could. No. It doesn't want to be free at all.

Let's say you meet someone who's free, or at least traveling very lightly. Then the mind will make them special. Because that will excuse you from the responsibility to be light. It's easy to want to be light, but to be light is a different story.

It is nothing to be secure about. There's no final knowledge or ultimate understanding. No mystery to make of it. In that "I don't know" is the true security. There is a letting go. Nothing to grab on to. You don't have any clue how things are happening.

After a while, if the mind stops, you'll recognize the mental hands that were always grasping are actually wings you have to start navigating the unknown.

It's like a mirage. You see what looks like water but when you arrive there's no water there. We keep on seeing it a hundred miles farther on, the same optical illusion. The mind will keep on presenting it, it will still appear; only now you'll know it's not real.

A statement ascribed to Buddha is: "Events happen. Deeds are done. But there is no individual doer thereof."

There is no doer. But the mind harvests the sense of being a doer from doing. From having things go on through this apparatus. The favorite fields are the ones to which the most meaning is given — harvesting the sense of being the one doing something.

Events are happening and deeds are going to be done, but that does not imply that there is an individual doer. That's what's made up. The big leap in the mental process is, "I'm the one that's doing it." That's a huge leap. And if you look at it, really look at it, you see it's full of holes. The sense of being a doer implies control.

Okay. If you're in control: Stop thinking!

You are a thought in and of itself. You are a thought in the mental realm that's being identified with a body and a feeling and that's what makes up the illusion of being a long-lasting independent separate entity. It's a mental product that's occurring. And there's many gaps when it's not producing its effect when you sense a presence that has nothing to do with you. Yet the mind has the ability to deny it very well. It goes over a miracle like a speed bump. A minor interruption to its linear story.

The mind has fallen in love with the mental process it has made. It's very interested in the "you" and having the you continue. Interest is channeled into this apparatus and it's causing a good deal of perversity, neuroses. How could it not? All this energy focused on this one little object and one little mental realm called time. It's too much juice.

The thoughts aren't yours. They just come up from the conditionality of the apparatus.

There is a subservience to the mental realm. The mind is re-presenting conscious contact as you being the one that's conscious, which is causing a total experience of unconsciousness.

Totally unconscious to the fact that we are ocean. All day, totally in the appearance of being a wave. The life of a wave represented constantly. I could have been bigger, I should have been smaller. I should've picked up that shell. It goes on and on. Your interest is absorbed in it. What's going to happen to me? Unbelievable. All the attention thrown into me.

What do you need to do about it? Absolutely nothing. Just become awake to it. Entertain it. Hey, is that actually going on? You have the ability to see. The ability to recognize an illusion as an illusion. The reality of the illusion is based on your believing it.

You have the ability to download other than this mental realm all day.

In martial arts there is the concept of "no mind." One trains and trains for the body to perform actions automatically, without thinking about them.

Since the time I was a kid, if something dropped I could catch it; my hand-eye coordination was really good. There is no thinking involved. Like the way I caught the mashed potatoes today. Just a reaction.

But you don't have to train for it. It's a quality you can exercise now. How? Just the recognition, there isn't a you.

In earlier days I wanted to be Chinese. A Chinese tai chi master. I studied tai chi for a long time. I had this mythical idea of what it would be like to stay above everything. Be a man of the five talents. I was into it. I had a lot of intent. That mythical idea of the sage. My mind was really into that.

Totally bogus, as I think back on it. It was just insane.

Invite people to entertain what's already so. Sometimes a simple recognition, and the mind can become unravelled from the contortion of selfing. It can spring open, achieve its true size. Not the size of the body. Not the size of mind.

Someone finally dropped this little idea on me. I entertained it. Something radically slapped my head, and I paused. Sat there and kind of let it go through. The possibility of what I was was actually demonstrated in the entertaining.

It's really about getting disarmed, all your little mechanisms. Putting down the grasping. Noticing what's obvious. Because the mind says, "I'm seeing," that doesn't mean that's true. Just a mental process claiming the seeing.

The little mind claims the big mind. The big mind is not affected by that, it's just seeing. Always available at all times. No matter how much clinging, how much claiming you do, the one moment it's entertained not to be you, it all stops.

It's not like there's tons of years that have to be erased. It's just "pop." When you see something that you took to be real, and you see it as unreal, it's immediately unreal. No efforting.

After that? Seeing begets seeing.

Now I'll give you the secret answer . . .

But no, you haven't done enough yet. You have to go home and DO MORE.

Ha, ha, ha!

There's no work to entertaining what's so. Simply tell the truth about what's not so.

Once you see that...what's not so... Boom, that's entertaining what's SO. There's no work involved.

Now every time the selfing presents you handcuffs and you could so easily put them on — you don't. You don't give your wrists to it. You're free. Each moment free, free, free, free, free, free.

It's very freeing to entertain what's so.

The dilemma is that we are approaching what we are as what we're not. That's why it's hard to "arrive," because you cannot approach what you are from what you're not. You just have to look at what you're not, to see it's not you.

It has nothing to do with time or processing. What causes it to take time is that there is a "you" that's attempting to know the truth. But the truth is, there is no you.

If there is no you, what are you left with? You're left with the truth. Which is the act of seeing, right now. Consciousness, now.

Something is recognizing a "me." But the vehicle for that recognition is consciousness. You can become conscious of what you're not.

The act of seeing is what I am. That fact of being conscious. So what I am is not a noun that's conscious, it's a verb. Being conscious, that's what I am.

The mental process is what produces a sense of being a self.

You didn't have a sense of self when you were a baby. The first year and a half after birth there is no sense of you or other yet. All there is is consciousness. The brain is still under development.

Consciousness is activating the apparatus, but all the wiring hasn't been connected yet. Finally, in a year and a half or so, one of the mental processes produces the sense of being a self. The mental process asks, "Who am I?" And it gives itself the answer: I am what's easily recognized, the body. Then I became the body in a sense.

Once the I becomes the body it becomes who I primarily am. And if I am this, the body, how can I be spirit? The best I can do is to become "spiritual" AS a body. And the brain is the body, remember.

So with an identification with the body, it becomes my primary reference point or location. From this location I'm obviously not spirit so I have to "get spiritual." And usually I'll arrive at this point after I've tried to get other things. Get successful, get healthy, get my dream.

But getting the outside circumstances just right won't translate into happiness. Something's missing. So you come to one of the last houses on the block, which is spirituality.

The last gasp method: I'll become spiritual. I'll find a practice to do just that. I as this body am going to become spiritual by doing and having, which is the modality of self centeredness.

In doing and having I take myself to be something already and I do and have to create change, to amplify or decrease. I am like an urban renewal project being constantly looked over and supervised. "What do I need now? What could give me an advantage so that I could be doing better?" I as this, the body.

The primary identification becomes the starting point. From here the best I can do is to "become" spiritual by practicing things. Usually the first thing to do is to look spiritual. Practice the loving gaze. Talk more slowly. Pour out the feeling. Intone, "All is one."

But this is all malarkey. Because what is claiming itself to be one is defined by two-ness. There is no sense of being a self without the sense of another. There is no self without other. It's two-ness attempting to be one-ness. But two-ness can never become one-ness. It's a matter of a recognizing there is no two-ness. It's a totally different approach, yes?

So here you are as this (the body). The sense of being a self. It's felt. You feel as though you were the one having this feeling. You feel like you're the thinker. That you are different from another person because you can see her as being different from you as a body. And this difference the body demonstrates is now given to the quality of thought and feelings represented by the word "my."

Whatever you're looking at is being brought to you by seeing. If we went around the room and asked what was happening everyone would say, "I'm seeing you." In this case I'd be the you that all of you are seeing if you're looking this way. All the activity would be seeing. The sense would be that you are seeing and that what you're seeing is me, which is a "you" to you.

If we ask who is seeing, you say, "I'm seeing." There is a act of seeing and there's a feeling that I must be the one that seeing. This is the sense of a self.

The seeing is correct. But the sense that there is a Paul who is seeing is not. That is the mental addition to the act of seeing.

So here's the seeing, and I'm seeing you. If I ask who's seeing, I'd say, "I'm seeing." Okay. Now I ask again, who is this "I" that is seeing? Usually the answer will be, "Me." What is that me-part of the mental process?

When you're looking at me, I'm a you. I'm an object called a you. When I'm identified with this object called a you, it's a me.

So there is seeing: I, I, I, I. Everyone is on the right track. It's "I" that's seeing. In the experience of each of those present, what is seeing Paul is what I call spirit.

The mental process says, "All right, I'm going to ask who's seeing Paul. I'm seeing Paul." **The mental process claims it and becomes the I, the I that is a body. Therefore a me.**

If you consider your thinking, the mental process holds you as a body. When you think about you in the past how do you think about you? As a body, yes? When you think about you in the future, you're pictured as a body.

When you have a mental picture or prediction about what is possibly going to happen in the future, what is that you that it is going to happen to? The body. That is what the mental process holds as you.

The highest level that the thinking system can bring you to is you as a body. If you're relying on the system of thought, which most of us are, you're going to be identified with what it's identified as, which is a body. Seeing won't be noted as seeing, it will be "I'm seeing."

First there's simple seeing. So let's say a bird flies by the window. I see the bird if my eyes are open. My head may say, "I don't want to see that bird." But I saw the bird. That's conscious contact. That comes first.

The mental process says, I'm the one that does the seeing, tasting, touching. It says, **I'm going to step behind the consciousness, and I'm going to make spirit into a verb that "I am doing."** So I'm the one that is seeing. I'm the one that's feeling. I'm the one that's touching.

And then the mental process, having claimed the conscious contact riffs on it, playing God. I didn't want to feel that. I don't like that. I really want this, I don't like that. And it starts going off. Desires and aversions arise. Moving toward things you like and away from things you don't. Living a total interpretation of conscious contact by the mind.

When you were young you had many moments of wonder and awe.

Just give you a few toys and you could entertain thousands of possibilities with them. What happened? What happened to that wonder and awe, to that immediacy?

You were here because you weren't entertaining a there yet.

What's happened is we've been entertaining a there so long it's become here for us. Literally. We take what's not happening to be truly what's happening. Next Friday's concerns and worries become more important than the immediacy of this moment. Because we are sitting here occupied not by the conscious contact but by what's not happening.

The thoughts are about next week and what could possibly happen to you as a body. There is a large amount of concern about that. Your attention thrives on what's not happening, then you get constipated in a way, you can't come out. So now you're seeking relief from self as self. Self can't get out of self; how can the product of a mental process ever transcend the mental process? How can something that's made up, the feeling of being you, ever leave what produces the feeling of being you?

If your attention left the mental process, if you weren't so addicted to the idea of being a self, if your attention could entertain, "Possibly I'm not this that I'm so absorbed in and as," you would see there is no need to get out of self because there was never a self to be in.

No matter how real it seems to be, the effect it has is only on other appearances. If I hit this wall my arm is going to be hurt. So I think the wall is real because it produces a real effect on what I take to be real. What happens if, just maybe, this is an appearance in the reality of spirit?

The mental activity of selfing plays God here. It says, I've forgotten that all there is is consciousness, and consciousness is now an attribute that I can have or not have. I can be really conscious if I practice and meditate; or can be really unconscious if I eat ice cream and watch videos all night. So now consciousness, which is a prior state to everything that is appearing, is now a quality that you can have.

So you believe that you have achieved consciousness. What is immediately entertained if you believe you have achieved something? That you can lose it. Immediately. Immediately! The mind is dualistic, so that if it believes it can attain something it knows it can lose it.

But if you are it you can't lose it. It's totally taken out of the realm of the mind's god-playing. Because it's prior to what is playing god. It's always so, available at all times, with no requirement necessary.

Freedom is prior to any bondage, not after bondage.

If consciousness is all there is, it's the field of every where-ness in which appearances are rising.

Why are we taking ourselves to be what's appearing rather than what's noting the appearance? Why are we neglecting our true nature which is seeing? Not what's said to be the seer, but what's seeing, the act of seeing that is prior to everything that appears here, the consciousness that is prior to the mental reaction that is claiming it.

The Sheep and the Lion.

The Sheep and the Lion is an old Hindu story.

There was a mother lion with her cub. The mother dies and the cub is on its own. It's wandering around the savannah and it comes upon a flock of sheep.

At this point it has no idea of what it is. But the sheep know what it is and when it moves toward the sheep they get a little nervous. Though they quickly realize the lion has no bad intentions.

The flock accepts the lion, which begins to live as though it is a sheep. It tries to baaa, has concern about becoming a sweater and so on. Time goes by and the lion is well respected in the flock. Is even considering taking a mate.

Then one day another lion, an old one, gives chase to the sheep. As he nears he sees the young lion. Thinking it is joining him in the hunt he continues the chase, but soon realizes the young lion is running away from him along with the sheep.

The old lion veers off and grabs the young lion. The young lion is begging for mercy, crying out, "I'm just a humble sheep."

Saying nothing, the old lion drags the young lion to the water hole so they can both see their reflection. Seeing their faces together the young lion wakes up. The old lion says, "Roar." And the young lion roars. He doesn't need to take a three-month course of roaring. The ability was always innately there.

He has recognized, he is not a sheep.

Becoming a Lion When You're Already a Lion

Suppose I am a lion. But I am identified as a sheep; so that when I hear the message that I am a lion my head translates it as, "I can become like a lion."

Meanwhile I think I am a sheep; and I may desire the quality of lion-hood in order to become a better sheep.

We are lions but identifying ourselves as sheep we are under a huge amount of stress. Concerned about being herded, our hair being used for sweaters, and being taken away for food.

Maybe a couple of us aren't happy with this situation of being sheep. We come upon an old book about lions. We read, "The lion is the king of the jungle. Very courageous." That excites us. Qualities we desire that we believe we lack.

"I want to become like a lion!" They rent a hall. They find pictures of lions and place them in beautiful frames and light candles. They start having meetings to read about the lion and the way it roars. They try to act like lions. Practice roaring. Straighten their hair.

All well and good. But they are lions mistaking themselves as sheep. In this condition the only way they can entertain "lion" is to become "like" one. They cannot entertain their own lion-ness because they are identified as sheep.

This is the dilemma. You may like the message that you are a lion; but you are hearing it with sheep ears.

We take ourselves to be a body; then we hear we are not a body, but we hear it from the body's point of view. The body cannot imagine itself out of the equation. The body is the reference point and whatever comes through comes through that reference. If Spirit comes though it's seen as coming through the body. The reference point. It's a very strong habit. So hearing the message I am a lion, as a sheep, it can only become "like a lion," because the sheep is in that space. The stubbornness of the sheep mentality is impervious to attack.

A Note from Paul:
The Here There Syndrome

I wake up in my one bedroom apartment feeling pretty good have a nice latte waiting for me I have money in the bank a girlfriend, good car everything is fine feel pretty content. I'm leafing through a magazine on my coffee table and I see this full-page color advertisement for a nice lovely couch start looking around my room I realize I don't have a couch. start wondering what it would mean to me if I did have a couch maybe I'd meet a girl ask her over and conceive my first child on the couch. I could have a lot more people over and of course that would always be great. suddenly I realize life sucks without a couch. my contentment is now out the window. I want a couch. I cut the picture out and start counting the days till I get the couch. Call my friends to share my enthusiasm they don't seem to be as excited as I am. Order the couch and circle the day of it's arrival on the calendar. I can't wait. The day of the couch dawns. I sweep it's docking slip. Call some friends to come witness the event (they don't come) the men bring the couch in and what a couch. They set it down and leave me alone with the couch. I have it now all will be well. I start looking around my place and I suddenly realize I need a rug and so it goes. I entertain how great a there would be while invalidating the here I'm in. I work so hard to get that there. Only to realize when I arrive it's a here.

Your comments are welcome!

James Saint Cloud, Publisher
Email: Rumistories@ yahoo.com

Let It Be Publishing
4460 Redwood Highway #16-227
San Rafael, California 94903 USA

Notes

Notes